MARK O'ROWE

Mark O'Rowe began writing in 1994. After several youth
theatre productions, *From Both Hips* was produced by
Fishamble and won the Stewart Parker BBC radio drama
award. It is published in a volume with his first full-length
play, *The Aspidistra Code*. His third play, *Howie the Rookie*,
was first performed at the Bush Theatre, London.

He was born in Dublin and still lives there.

Mark O'Rowe

HOWIE
THE ROOKIE

NICK HERN BOOKS
London

A Nick Hern Book

Howie the Rookie first published in Great Britain in 1999
as a paperback original by Nick Hern Books Limited,
14 Larden Road, London W3 7ST

Front cover image courtesy of the Bush Theatre, London

Typeset by Country Setting, Kingsdown, Kent CT14 8ES
Printed and bound in Great Britain by Athenaeum Press, Gateshead

ISBN 185459 422 2

A CIP catalogue record for this book is available from the British
Library

For my parents
Hugh and Patricia O'Rowe

Howie the Rookie was first performed at the Bush Theatre, London on 10 February 1999, with the following cast. Press night was 12 February 1999.

THE HOWIE LEE	Aidan Kelly
THE ROOKIE LEE	Karl Shiels

Directed by Mike Bradwell
Designed by Es Devlin
Lighting by Simon Bennison

PART ONE

The Howie Lee

Smoke.

Black smoke ahead there, north end of the field.

Thick, billowin', curlin' up.

Somethin' burnin'.

Me, The Howie, south end, amblin'.

Approachin'.

A figure.

A man ahead, some fuck standin' there, stick in his hand, proddin' whatever's burnin'. Makin' sure it all goes up.

Me, The Howie Lee, getting' closer now.

Passin' through the field, me way home.

Field, the back of the flats there, back of Ollie's flat, me mate Ollie's an', Jesus, it *is* Ollie, little fire built, he's standin' there, watchin' it, one hand in his pocket, now an' again, stick prods the burnin' . . . whatsit?

What *is* it?

Come close. All right, Ollie?
All right, The Howie?
Stop, stand, cock me tush.
The fuck're you burnin'?
Me mat, he says.

Ollie's flat befits a messy cunt like him.
Kip the night, you kip on the guest mat under an oul' slumber-down. You're a bloke and you're game, you can kip in the bed *with* him. Game meaning gay, neither of which I am, furthest

thing from, so I go the mat. Or did.
On the mat, I kip.

Did! Kipped!
It's gone, now. That's it he's burnin'.

Burnin' the quilt as well, so if you want to kip over, the future,
only place is the single bed, now, you spoonin' him or him
spoonin' you, neither of which, like, fuck both of which, 'cos I
don't like either.

Me mat's gone, he says. Me mat's burnin'.
'Cos it's got a disease and it can't be slept on.
'Cos it's got scabies.
Scabies?
Mat's got scabies, *I've* got scabies, he says. I've this cream on
me, I've all over me body. Have to leave it for twenty-four
hours, have to burn me mat.

Itchy? I asks him.
Itchy all over, he says. Are you itchy, a-tall?
Haven't slept on your mat in while, now.
Lucky you, he says. Wouldn't wish it upon you.

Adios, Ollie, says I. Adios, The Howie, then home.
Keys out, front door, open an' in, ignorin' everyone, The Howie
this, that, The Howie, fuck youse.

Up to me bedroom, slide the bolt of privacy an' peace.

Peace and quiet, nice.

Dirty rags, polish me tool, nice one.

Lie back, catnap an' repose.

Bangin' on me door, the oul' one, wake up, she's fuckin'
poundin' on me door.
Get off the bed, over, slide the bolt an' out the landin', swayin'
left an' right, the sudden rush of blood to me head. The oul'
one standin' there, bad breath, ugly, dresses nineteen-fifties pop
sock teenybopper, very few grey cells, the oul'fella's even less,
he does as she says, not because she's powerful, no, not
because he's scared of her . . .

Tom?! The oul'fella. Tom?!

What?
You comin' up the fort?

Yeah.
. . . But because he's nothin' better to do.
Nothin' better, 'cos he *knows* no better.

You're wanted on the phone, she tells me.

Pick up, it's Ollie.
Ollie with the mat, who I met.

C'mere, he says. Me an' The Peaches is after someone. Would
you like to be after someone with us?
Who're youse after? I says. I asks.
Someone you'll like bein' after, but someone who I can't tell
you, 'cos of The Peaches, he says. 'Cos it's The Peaches'
fuckin' skit.

Ah, now, this is all a bit fuckin' skullduggerous, I says.

But, it's The Peaches' *skit*, he says. Call up to me after.
After me dinner?
Yeah.
Right. But, what's up?
After your dinner.

Hang up, smell of carrots an' parsnips. Lovely.

Bit of bad, now, bit of hassle, the oul' one.
Tryin' to eat me dinner, sittin', she's at me.
At me goodo, she's in me face; pop socks an' cardigan.

Mind your brother. Mind Mousey.
I'm busy.
Me an' your oul'fella's goin' the fort.
I'm busy, get out of me face.

Wears this spangly glitter shit on her cheeks, 'cross her nose,
her glasses magnify, make it flash at me, gimme a tense
nervous.

I won't get out of your face.
Leave me alone.
No, I *won't*. You *mind* The Mousey Lee.
No, I won't.

So forth, enter the oul'fella.

Cycles fifteen miles to work and back every day.
Got a bad ticker, was told take it easy or die, so he saved for a car.
Saved, went without, like, sacrificed.
Walkin' by Harry Moore's one day, saw a handicam.
Now, has the handicam, fuck the car.
Fuck the ticker, fuck his life, full fuckin' stop.

She's standin' over me, naggin', *he's* standin' over the two of us, handicam perched, red light flashin', the record light, tense nervous becomes migraine.

Carrots an' parsnips in the bin.
No, no, no I won't. No, I *won't* mind The Mouse.

Up the jacks.
Up, shower, freezin', cold enough to stop me heart – I love it – dressed an' down.

Mousey.

There's The Mousey Lee, kitchen now, sittin' on an armchair, watchin' me.
I say, I'm sorry, I'm busy, (feel a bit guilty.) I can't, man.

Mousey's five, he just started school.

Do you understand, The Mouse? I've business.
He does, he under . . . *'Course* he understands, he's the brother, you know?

He's the fuckin' brud, he is.

Out the front door, oul' one behind me, oul'fella behind her.
Trip on the step, I go on me snot.
Side of the road, I'm out on me snot, oul'fella's gigglin' like a youngfella, he got me goodo, got me on video.
I'm down, change rollin' round, silver an' copper, fuck it, he's comin' towards me, now, red light flashin'.
Up, go.
Come back, he says.
Fuck that.
Come back for your money.

He's laughin' hyena style, she's not, she's mad. Mad in both, mad in *all* senses.

Fuck the money.

Call up to Ollie's.

Ollie comes out, call up to Peaches'.

Not in the best of moods, Peaches, have to say. Big dirty puss on him.
I wanna know why we're here, his oul'one's kitchen, but it's his skit an' he wants to go out first.

Bein' teased righteous, I am, 'cos they know I'm a curious fucker.

Delayin' me, they are.
Delayin' me earlier, delayin' me now.

Tell me somethin' first.
We go out first.
A *morsel*, man. Tell me who the fuck we're after.

After someone, you're lookin' for them. Gonna give them a hidin', hurt them, you're chasin' them.
Someone's after you, you're hunted.

Tells me we're after The Rookie Lee.

Nice one, says I. Thank you. I enjoy bein' after people. Thanks for tellin' me. 'Specially . . . (*At last.*) 'Specially cunts like The Rookie Lee. Handsome cunts. 'Specially cunts with the same last name as me.

Lee as in The Bruce.

So, we're after The Rookie righteous.
Why, Peaches?
After.
Goes for a piss before departure.

Don't flush, I says.

Out he goes, in comes Avalanche. A monster. Peaches' sister.
Sixteen stone, size forties on her chest, few tats.
She's askin' can she come with us.

Not tonight, sister.

She belches in Ollie's face, midsentence, Jaysus, doesn't even know she does it. She's talkin' 'bout gettin' a *new* tat – A tat on me gat, she says – Ollie's tryin' to keep his head averted, breathe through his mouth, he doesn't get the bile stink off her breath.

Jacks flushes, in comes Peaches. Nice one, Peaches.
Bollox! he says.
Nice one for flushin' the jacks, now I've to flush it *again* . . .
Bollox! he says.
. . . waste *more* fuckin' water.

Aahhhh!

Flood from me cock. Piss. A nice one.
Footsteps on the stairs, someone behind me.
I know who.
A hand on me business, Jaysus, holdin' it.
I know who.
Aimin' it for me, shakin' the last drops.

Avalanche.

Had her once, have to say.

Starts pullin' me off bandy, wringin' me flute.

Fuck it, tell the truth, I had her three times and dug it to fuck. Far as she's concerned, sexual prowess, you know, fuckin' tech*nique* is measured in poundage an' far as . . . or stonage . . . fuckin' *ton*nage, an' far as I'm concerned, she's right 'cos I've been there and I've measured and had that good time and *been*, you know, that fuckin' scales, 'cos I let *her* go on top.

Oh, yeah.

One of these days, she'll kill me an' I won't mind a fuckin' bit.

Whisperin' in me ear, now, askin' me to come into her bedroom.
No, I says. Shut up or your brud'll hear.
Slip into me room an' slip into me womb, she says.
Shut the fuck up, I says, take her hand off me flute.

Tells me she's gonna be in Flahertys in town 'til late if I wanna hook up. Say I'll see. Say if I manage to slip away. Good enough for her. Off she goes, down the sittin' room, her grotesque arse bet into a pair of ski pants – not the white ones, thank Jaysus, see her piss-flaps an' everything – the *black* ones, down the stairs and out of me sight.

Back the kitchen go I.
Me an' Ollie, no Peaches, where's Peaches?

Have Patience, The Howie. Peaches is ill, says Ollie. He's a bit weak.
Oh. What?!
He's not in the best, you'll find out why. Just let him go at his own pace.

More skullduggery.

Enter The Peaches, youse right?
Enter The Peaches, *vamonos*, he says, exit the boys, passin' the sittin' room on the way, Avalanche lettin' rip a nice one – a belch, like, not a fart – loud enough we hear it through the door.

Into the streets, Rookie Lee's gaff bound, *after* him, you see, not too far.
Knock, not in, no lights, where?
Knock, no answer, where?

Up the new shops.
Call them the new shops the last ten years, 'cos ten years ago, when they were built, that's what we called them *then*. Built in a circle, their backs face out to keep bandits at bay.

Rookie Lee sometimes hangs 'round Video Vendetta video rentals. He's not there, so we sit on the wall an' we smoke.

Might still turn up.

Two smokes. Three. Four for Ollie – God bless his lungs – still no sign.

Sittin' there, spot an oul'one goin' in the Vendetta, stall it boys, follow her in, this oul'one, arm in a cast, stitches in her face, name's Susan.

My oul'one knows her, calls her *Skip* Susan.

All right, Susan?
All right, she says.

Crashed her car into a wall, few weeks ago.

Gards an' firemen pulled up, car was wrecked, but she wasn't
in it.

Men were sent to look around the area, see if she was
wanderin' 'round, delirious or somethin'.

Was an hour 'fore someone thought about lookin' in the big
yellow skip was behind the wall an' there she was all wrecked
to bits, unconscious. Must've wandered off an' climbed in.

Shock, you know?

Poor woman had no insurance, nothin'. Damaged herself a bit
financially too. She's off work, single, not too mobile.

D'you wanna babysit for me brud? I says. For The Mousey
Lee?
Bit of charity, you see?
The oul'one an' oul'fella's goin' down the fort, need someone
to mind him.
Em . . . she says.
Your decision, man, I says, you want a penny or two.
Ring the gaff 'fore half eight, I says, writes the number on her
cast. You can watch your video there. Winks at her stylish.
Few bob in it for you.

Back the wall.
Peaches, Ollie an' me perched.
Peaches, Ollie says. Peaches. D'you wanna . . .? Bein' gentle
with him, now, talkin' softly.
. . . D'you wanna tell The Howie your story, now?

Peaches tells us a story.

This is what I've been . . . Yep. At last. Story they were holdin'
back from me.

At fuckin' last.

A funny story, but sad. Feel sorry for him, I do.

'Cos, see, he slept on Ollie's mat too. Only he went to his

doctor, 'stead of just going to a chemist, gettin' the scabie cream. Went to the doctor, this packie dirtbird, Coovadia and Coovadia gave him this *other* stuff, this black and white days cruel muck, burned the poor fucker up.

Gave him torments, it did.

Peaches senior, the old man, found him lyin' on the jacks floor in his nip, bollox shaved to bits – doctor dirtbird told him to shave it – he's screamin' his head off, rolling around asking to be put down like a dog.

Like a fuckin' mungrel!

Shaved bollox is the funny bit. Torments of hell's, I think's the sad bit. Askin' to be put down like a dog's just pathetic. His oul'fella filled the bath with freezin' water, put him in and left him there for an hour 'til his skin stopped burnin'.

The whole process left poor Peaches a bit fuckin' drained to say the least. Even to look at him now . . .

An' his oul'fella saw his shaved bollox.

This is the bit that depresses The Peaches the most.

It depresses me as well. Someone has to pay for The Peaches' sufferin' an' shame an' The Rookie, me namesake in Lee-ness, was the last person before him, he tells us, to sleep on that mat. One night after a party, he asked Ollie could he kip in his place, the neck, the dirty *neck* on him. Ollie couldn't say no, 'cos Ollie's bent an' The Rookie's sexy, thought he'd get him into the sack, give him a ridin', but straight Rookie, *hetero* Rookie, chose the mat.

An' if he was the last person to sleep on it, then he either caught the scabies *off* it or gave the scabies *to* it.

If he caught it, he would've said something, he would've warned us and he didn't.

He kept his fuckin' mouth shut.

Which means he infected it.

Which means he infected the boys.

Which means we're after him, the handsome cunt.

A green hi-ace van pulls in the car park, Flann Dingle and
Ginger Boy jump out.
Flann Dingle's fat and sweaty, Ginger Boy's short, ginger hair,
red enough it could stop traffic.

All right, lads? We know them.
In they go, the Vendetta, new release/action adventure.

Out they come – John Woo, Last Hurrah for Chivalry – ask us
we wanna come down the Mercy loop, mile an' a half, snakin'
road, watch Ginger Boy surf on the roof.
Peaches doesn't, he's not in the best, wants to conserve his
strength for batterin' The Rookie.
Well, d'you mind waitin', The Peaches? 'Course he doesn't.
You spot The Rookie, keep him talkin'.
Be back in a quick.

Ginger Boy gets on the roof an' shouts, Punch it, Flann
Dingle! an'*vamonos!* down the Mercy.

We hang out the side door, lookin' up at Ginger Boy.

What d'youse think? asks Flann, all perspiry behind the wheel.
Very good, we say; our heads all windswept. *Very* good.

Funny thing's we're probably in a more dangerous position
than Ginger Boy, two of us hangin' out the side door, swerve to
avoid the one two three bus, tryin' to get an eyeful of the little
fuck dicin' with a flattenin'.

Bottom of the loop, hang a U, Ginger Boy grabbin' the roof
rack for dear life an' back up we go, this time sittin' in*side* the
van, 'stead of hangin' out the side door, two thick monkeys.
But we're thick monkeys for *getting'* in the van in the *first*
place, we're tryin' not to retch, 'cos sweaty Flann Dingle's the
essence of stench. Stinkball like him.

Fuckin' dung-beetle.

Deposit us, Flann Dingle. Deposit us up the new shops 'fore
I'm sick. (not to his face, now.) No wonder Ginger boy travels
on the roof. (to ourselves.) No wonder Peaches didn't come.

That a . . .? That a . . .? What's that? That The Rookie Lee?
Where? Stop, stop the van. Stop the van, that's The Rookie at
the bus stop, stop.

Flann Dingle stops. Doesn't stop, Ginger boy's on top. Doesn't
stop, slows down. Out the back window, sketch! whatsit, aaagh
fuck! a bus, a bus, the one two three, he's getting' on, he gets
on, he's goin' to town. Into town, all the way, fuck! Peaches,
standin' there beside the bus-stop, watchin' him get on, doin' a
dance, a shimmy-shuffle of indecision, left to right an' back,
doesn't know whether to follow or wait, so waits.

Let us out, Flann Dingle, give us some fresh air, (in our minds,
now.) let's away from your stench (not to his face.).

Deposited.

Alone. Green hi-ace pissed off.

Waitin'.

Waitin', sayin' *typical*. You leave a place for five fuckin'
minutes, fuckin' *typical*.
Rookie on the bus, town bound.
But . . .
Typical.
But . . .
What?
Asked him where he was goin', didn't I? says The Peaches,
pleased as punch.
Asked him his destination an' he told me Chopper's. Chopper
Al's of Lime street. Amen't I good? Amen't I clever?

He's *very* fuckin' clever.

Pass the time, Ollie starts goin' on about how a strong body
odour can be attractive in a man. Not in Flann *Dingle*, say, but
in *some* men. I don't wanna hear. Peaches is interested, asks
lots of questions. Clarifies. In a better mood, now, 'cos he's a
bead on the Rookie, we've a bearin'.

Wonderin' if Skip Susan rang the gaff.

One two three, nice one.
Boardin', boardin', down the back, seats facin', feet up.

Bus driver's fast, he wants his tea. Twenty K, twenty minutes flat. Nice.
Alightin', alightin', Dame street deposited.

People meetin', standin' 'round, yappin', strollin', chinwaggin'. Out of the way, we've no time, we're on business. We're forgin' ahead, excuse us. But enjoy yourselves all the same. Don't mind us.

Shortest distance between two points is a straight line, but since we can't walk through walls an' buildin's, it's up Rowney Street – all right, Peaches? I am – right at the green, left an' right down Lime Street, Chopper Al's, what's the plan?

Ah, the plan.

Pretend we're his mates.

Pretend we're not after him. Sup a couple, nab him outside after so's not to rumble 'front of The Chopper.

Enjoy ourselves.

Yeah, Peaches?
Fine, he says.

And then we make our move.

In we go, so, spot The Rookie an' two birds, dolly birds, blackie and blondie – their *hair*, like – sit down, no invite, fuck that.

All right, The Rookie Lee? says I, all right, me namesake?

A good move, that. A social move.
You me an' The Bruce Lee.

Peaches orders. Up the bar, probably wants to steel himself a bit, his emotions before he sits down, faces the man caused all his pain an' shame.

Blackie an' blondie. Dolly, they are, think The Rookie Lee's the bee's knees, little does the bee's knees realise, he's not getting' his hole tonight.

Neither blackie *nor* blondie he's getting'.

A *hidin'*, he's getting' for what he done to The Peaches.

Peaches returns. Pints for the boys, we socialise.

Startin' to feel a bit embarrassed, though.
Bit uptight in meself. Not talkin' much, leave it to Ollie.
Bein' a faggot, he doesn't get overwhelmed by the dollyness.

Chattin' away there, charmin' fucker *like* him.

Lack of success with birds, I have.
Have to say . . .
Hence, fuckin' whatser . . . Avalanche.

An' I keep catchin' the blondie one's eye, for fuck's sake.
Every time I look at her – shite! – she looks at me the exact
same time.

Probably thinks I'm after her.
(The romantic sense, like, not the other . . . the batterin'.)

Look at her again, she catches me eye again.

Look at her again an' . . . Fuckin' *hell!*

Look to me left an' The Rookie's doin' somethin' similar, 'cept
he's wired, observant, head cocked, cuttin' his eyes me
direction. Look and his eyes twitch away.

D'youse want another pint? he asks us.
Are you buyin'?
No, he says, but I'm goin' up.
We give him money, he goes up.

Ollie goes the jacks.

Me, Peaches, blondie and darkie, all a-circle.

I'm quiet, feel shy without Ollie's gab.

Dollys start talkin' among themselves. Good.

Go to say somethin' to Peaches, but he's lookin' towards the bar.
Lookin' up at The Rookie.

Not lookin', no.

Starin'.

Rememberin' the shame, his oul'fella, I can see it, the scabies'
pain.

Dollys stop talkin', go quiet.
Dollys can see it too, can sense it.

Rookie at the bar.

Peaches watchin', sneerin', givin' him the evil eye.

Rookie with the fidgets, itchy, tryin' not to scratch front of the
dollys.

All a-quick, Peaches can't hold it in anymore, explodes,
lunges, blindsides The Rookie. I stand up. Rookie lands against
the bar, Peaches lunges again, tries to sandbag him; fast an'
hard, but sloppy. Rookie dodges, picks a pint off the bar, fucks
it at us, dives over a table, but it's only a ha'penny dive an'he
lands on top. Booze pell-mell, scrambles off, beelines for the
door, he's out. But we're already runnin' across the table he
dove across, then out the door, spot him, up the street, after
him like The Christie; like The fuckin' Linford, flutes bouncin'
around heavy an' all, sprintin' righteous, sprintin' like the
Dickens, gainin'. We're gainin' goodo, gainin' ground, getting'
closer, movin', movin'. Down a lane he goes, best place to get
him – quiet, solitary – I make a final burst, power forward, me
lungs burn, me muscles boil, I pound ahead like a
thoroughbread, snortin' an' whinnyin'.

I dive.

Very smoothly. Nothin' ha'penny about *my* dive.
I'm like Tarzan.

I dive.

Like the fuckin' *Weismuller*, I am.

I dive, I sail, I take him down.
I take down my prey like a feral hunter and hold him tight as
Peaches runs up, huffy and puffy, three men standin', three
hearts poundin' loud, three lungs, pairs of lungs, suckin'
louder, suckin' hard.

Then softer, then calmer, then quieter.

Then quiet.

Peaches lays in.

Body shots, head shots, not too hard, have to say, gently
bruisin' the handsome cunt's ribs. Split lip, good one, swollen
eye swellin' up. The Rookie tries to defend himself. He's
feeble. I hold his arms anyway.
I hold his arms, but I'm a bit put off. Not really into it. Must
be all that runnin', me stomach's queasy.

Peaches finishes off with a right-left combo to the mush, right
hook to the darby.
Weak Rookie, battered Rookie drops, exhausted, Peaches
breathin' hard again.
Rookie's not too hurt, drops from the run, not the hidin'.
Peaches is weak, not much weight, but he's satisfied.
We got him.

Satisfied?
Yeah.
Back to Chopper's?
Let's go.

Ollie's standin' outside, forlorn, smokin'. Chopper Al fucked
him out after the hassle, after the fucked pints an' the
Weismullers 'cross tables. Pissed off he missed all the action,
pissed we went when he was havin' a shite, but what can we do?

Peaches is on a high, but. Vengeance exacted, look at him,
bouncin' up the street like a baby. Wants to go home, drop
down the fort, drink there so's he can just *roll* home, 'stead of
havin' to taxi or bus it.
Ollie concurs, tells Peaches it's a good deduction.

I concur with that deduction, he says.

But *I* don't concur. Don't concur a-tall.
For one, the oul' one an' oul'fella's in the fort.
For two, I'm feelin' horny. Me mickey's a bit sensitive and I'm
thinkin' 'bout Peaches' sister, Avalanche down Flaherty's.

'Course I don't say this, I say see youse tomorrow, boys, a job
well done an' off they go an' off *I* go.

Strollin' nice, lookin' forward, hopin' she's still down
Flaherty's, Flann Dingle an' Ginger boy swing past, green hi-
ace with the slidin' door open.

Shout over, Are you goin' home? Would you like a jaunt?
I wouldn't, says I. I'll stall it here, many thanks.

Off they go.
Mellow. No toolin'. Cruisin'.
It's that kind of night.

Continue me stroll.

Stop at a phone box, ring home.
Two rings, three, fou . . . almost four, pick up, hello?
It's Susan, Skip Susan, she took me up, went over, good one.
Chat with her a minute, everything all right?
He's a dote, she says, your brud, The Mousey Lee.
He is, I say. Happy, now.
Duty done, oul'one appeased.

Hang up, I continue me stroll, there's footsteps behind me,
runnin', tryin' to catch up, fuck's that? Spin 'round quicko,
Jaysus, it's blondie. Blondie from Chopper Al's. Catches up,
says her mate's gone home, am I goin' on? she says. I say I am.

Are you comin'?

Her nostril opens a bit.
I am, she says.

Jesus Christ!

This kinda thing doesn't happen very often, now.
Neither the invitation, *nor* the nostril.

Name's Bernie, she tells me. Sexier than Av, she gives me a
horn.
Name's The Howie Lee, I say.
I've a horn 'cos I've a chance, an invitation for you know what.
Unsaid at the time, but said. Implied. I can see it.

Implied with a flared nostril.

An' I know it's me machoness she's attracted to.
Me dangerousness.

Didn't find her sexy in the pub, 'cos I'd no chance. Find her
sexy now.

Stroll on lustful, me mickey followin' the beck of a nostril that widens an' says Let's.

Let's.

Did youse get The Rookie Lee? she asks me.
I say, We did. But got him gentle.
Says she'd like to've watched, 'cos she likes watchin' blokes scrappin'.

Ah-ha!

Were youse after him over the fishes? she says.
The fishes?
He said someone was after him over fishes.
Wasn't fuckin' *us*, I say. Is that why he was so nervous?
I don't know, she says, an' that's that.

That's all the interest she shows.

Must be one of them cold blooded dollys.

She links me arm an' we stroll on romantic.

Are you goin' to Dave McGee's bash tomorrow night? she says.

Fuckin' Dave McGee.

Rich Dave McGee went away, made his fortune, in the nuts an'
bolts makin' business, came back, built a huge gaff down
Canal way, just at the edge of the mountain, there.
Eleven months of the year, he travels, one, comes home,
throws a big, big bash for the whole town.
One an' all's invited.
One an' all goes.

I says, Are *you* goin'?
She says she is.
Well, then, I says, maybe *I* will, too.

An' I get the feelin' she wants me to.

We go to Reagan's.
Good. Once it's not Flaherty's.
Pint, a white wine spritzer, an' Bernie – have to remember her
name – she's lookin' a bit shitfaced, now, shitfaced but sexy, a
bit touchy, bit loosey-goosey.

Touchin' me leg, hand, thigh.
Talkin' close, sweet breath, bit boozy.

Jesus, hand on me leg, she's talkin' 'bout her brother she lives with, just the two of them, brother she takes care of 'cos he's sick. Askin' me do I understand? Brother she's looked after for years, works in her local Spar to provide for him.

Tell her that's respectable.

'Cos there's no-one else, she's responsible.

Tell her that's admirable.

An' she starts to go on . . .

Tells me she's savin' to put him in a special school for special people that he'll only get out of twice a month so she can live her *own* life and it's expensive and she works hard to save and she *deserves* a night out.

Bit resentful, now, must say. Resentful of her brud.

I says, Of *course* you deserve it.

She's on the tear tonight an' she's *goin'* to Dave McGee's party tomorrow an' that's all there is *to* it.

Bit fuckin' bitter.

You're right, I says.
That's all there is to it, she says.
You're fuckin' right.

An' on she goes . . .

There's a film John Wayne was in . . .

Was a western . . .

No.

An' on she goes anyway, an' who gives a fuck?
An' I'm getting' a pain in me hole.
Less loosey, now, have to say, feelin' a bit less goosey, 'cos I can't get a word in edgeways.

Another pint, another spritzer.
An' on she goes.

An' two more.

An' on she goes.

Into the jacks, *Jesus!*
Respite an' a heavy dribble.

Someone behind me, *Fuck* . . . in' hell, a soft warm belch, a
hand on me flute. I dry up, spin 'round, it's not a bloke, thank
Christ.

Not a bloke, but The Av.
Av in the gents, doin' that trick again, grabbin' me business,
the fuck did *you* come out of?

We ridin' tonight?
I'm with someone.
I saw her, she says, she's a pig.

I turn back, resume me interrupted stream of yellow.
Finish, shake, Av takes me aside.
If I don't fuck her tonight, she'll tell Peaches I fucked her
before. She's horny for me, she's jealous of Bernie; Bernie's
locks, looks, Bernie's figure, fuck.

I'll be in Flaherty's, she says an' she's gone.

So fuckin' disappointed!

Go out, tell Blondie, tell Bernie, Sorry, man, have to go. Have
business. Have to meet me mates, I says.
But, c'mere, I says, can I have your number? Give you a
shout?
You're not that good lookin', she says. Crushes me.
But I'm a good goer, I says.
You're not the *only* man, you know.
Look at her eyes. Bloodshot, unfocused, she's pissed.
. . . I'm scopin' this fuckin' bar while you're in the jacks, she
says, got the attention of *many* a horny fellow. *Many* a hunk
I've the attention of, now go away so's I can click, thank you
very much.

So, I go, hangin' me head, an' 'fore I reach the door, I hear a
thunk. A loud thunk. Loud enough I turn an' her head's on the
bar, her eyes closed, bit of blood, there, small trickle.

Looks like she cut herself.

Barman lifts his eyebrows at me as if to say, She with you?
Shrug me shoulders as if to say, You must be fuckin' jokin'.

Fuck her. She should be at home anyway.

Flaherty's.

A dirty dive. Av's type of place.
Place you can fuck in the jacks easy an' there she is at the bar,
arse enough for three stools, she's wearin' – good Jesus – the
white ski-pants, the see-through ones. I wanna do it now, get it
over with, 'cos I'm not in the mood any more. Could've had
somethin' good, 'stead of *this*.

Avalanche wants to have a pint first.

Fine, fine, we'll *have* a fuckin' pint.
But not said like that, now, said nice.

Drink our pints, I buy a snack bar an' munch it.

Smoochy music's playin', small dance floor, you can dance.
Av pulls me up, we dance, we waddle, only ones up.
Lots of wind in the Av tonight, rumblin's inside, belches over
me shoulder.
A dance, a shift. Open mouth splashers, I hold her close. Close
so's I can feel the belch in her chest risin', can stop kissin'
before it reaches her mouth.

Dancin' drunk, fuck, *too* drunk, trip over each other's feet, we
go down.
Ninnies over diddies, we're all acrumple, people lookin',
laughin', a sight we must be.

I'm gone off, tell her I'm goin' home.
Get up, help her up, tell her I'm tired. I've a migraine, forgive
me, tell her I don't feel too well. *Something*.

People still lookin', few still laughin'.

Don't know what's wrong with me tonight.
Feel strange in meself.
Feel like I'm goin' through some kind of change.

Want to go home.

She's upset, fuck her.
She feels unwanted, unloved, sorry 'bout you. Sorry 'bout you,
man, I've to go.
Goin' home, don't *want* a ride.
Couldn't get it up if I did.

When it suits you, she says, she shouts, when it suits you, that it?
Shoutin' at me, hysterical, I'm embarrassed doubleo now,
we're like a real live couple havin' a tiff.

As if.

Wanna turn to everyone in the bar an' say, Me an' her. As
fuckin' if, huh?

Dirty fat cunt like her.

An' on she goes, variations on when it suits you and storms
out, waddles up the street – Jesus, those ski pants – lurchin'
one side of the path to the other.

I get the one two three. Another driver wants his tea baddo,
fifteen minutes home.

Get home, I get in the door.
Get in the door, the oul' one's there, cryin'.

What's wrong with you, the oul' one?
Takes a while to answer, looks at me, snivels, says I'm a
bastard 'cos I wouldn't babysit. All I fucking need, I want peace.
Bastard 'cos I wouldn't babysit, 'cos Skip Susan had to
babysit.

Susan babysat, Susan fell asleep.

Mousey went out, let himself out, saw money at the edge of
the road.

Oh, no.

Saw money, wanted it. Coins.

Oh, no . . . Somethin's . . .

Silver an' copper.

Somethin's fuckin' comin'.

Night shift Sam 'cross the road, backin' his truck out, felt a bump. D'you understand?

You little hump, she calls me.

Felt a bump, stopped, came 'round, saw Mousey there, The little Mousey Lee, lyin' there, parts . . . parts of him crushed, you could see it. Dyin'.

You humpy cunt, she calls me.

Mousey, money still in his hand, she says. Know what he said?

Spangly glitter shit's runnin' down her face.

How much is that? he said. Held the money out, his little body broken to fuckin' bits, asked, How much is that?

Then he dropped the money 'cos he was crushed.

Crushed an' dead.

Your brother's dead, 'cos you wouldn't babysit, because you wouldn't do what you were told.

That can't be . . . Hang on . . .

'Cos you wouldn't do what you were told, she says.

That can't be right.

It's your fuckin' fault.

Shoutin' brings the oul'fella down, handicam at the ready. I dodge by him, push him aside, back out the front door, goin' on me snot the exact same spot I did earlier, expect laughs an' get fuck all.

Up straight away, get up an' move.

Oul' one an' oul'fella at the front door, but not laughin'.
Not laughin' this time.

Cryin'.

Don't look back.

It's your fuckin' fault.

It's your fuckin' fault.

Keep movin'. Get away. Get away from that house, that street.

It's your fuckin' fault.

The fuck can it be my fault?

PART TWO

The Rookie Lee

Oul'fella left us for this tramp, this ten years younger hooer could slicken up better than the oul'one.

Moved in with her treated her as his ever lovin', neglected me – the fuck – me sisters. The oul'one hit it hard then, whiskey an' vodka.

Thought it made him virile, he did, such a stud, but I showed him what a *real* stud is.

Down the fort one night, met the tramp, bought her a drink. Chatted, flattered, flirted, lured, seduced, *fucked* this dirty jezebel, stole the oul'fella from us.

Handsome bastard, I am. Bit attractive to the dollys, they're into me.
Find them easy to pick up, easy to get.
Break hearts an' hymens, I do.

Took her home the flat that night, ploughed her rapid, sent her away without her ninnies.

Followin' day, called up the oul'fella.

All right, son? he says.
These are your bird's, da, says I, holds out the dirty ninnies.
Left them in the flat last night when we were doin' it.
Doin' what? says he.
Doin' lodgy-bodgy, says I. Take a sniff. She was wet.

Haven't seen him in about twenty months, now.

I call up early.

Desperate.

Tramp answers. The oul'fella there? I say.

Go away, she says.
Da! I shouts.

Out he comes, lookin' haggard.
What do you want?
Money.
Do I look like I've money? he says, an' he doesn't. He looks
like a knacker.
How much are you lookin' for?
Five hundred quid, says I.
(*Snorts.*) Goes like that. (*Snorts.*) Now fuck off, he says, shuts
the door on me.

Walkin' away, the door opens again.

How's your oul'one?
She's good, I say. She's still doin' the courses.
Good, he says.
Better than you, you cocksucker.

Door slams, opens a*gain*.

The Rookie.
What?!!
Have you started seein' them pitbulls yet? he says.

Slams the door a final time.

When I was young, the oul'fella told me 'bout the ancient
Mayan Indians.
Mayans believed God of death shows himself to a man many
times before takin' him, like, before he dies.

One man might keep seein' a black panther if he lives in the
jungle, the same black panther.

Desert it might be a vulture or a particular camel or somethin'.

Vision here might be a . . . say a crow or a pitbull terrier.

So, see, when he said have you started seein' them pitbulls yet,
it meant, May you be dead soon, which is what I think of him
too, 'cept I desperately need some fuckin' money.

Down the fort for fortification, I'm in the jacks, checkin' me
wounds.

Black eye, split lip, scrapes, not too bad, that Peaches is a bit weak.

Him an' The Howie Lee, me namesake, givin' me the bates over who knows what?
Sort of thing can go on, *does* go on.
One minute, people's your buds, next, they're after you, some reason you don't know. Can happen, happens, goes on.

Probably think they got me baddo, the dirtbirds.
Didn't get me baddo a-tall, but.
Got me all right.
Got me such a way I've still me faculties.

Scared, but.

Last night was nothin' to what tonight might be.

Fuckin' itchin's getting' bad. Might have to go to Coovadia soon, tell me I've some kind of STD or somethin', laugh in me face.

It travels, it does. Was in me belly, now it's down between me leg an' me sack. Me bollox, itches the good thing.

Wash me hands an' go back in the pub.

Bushmills an' ice, please, John. Good bloke. Sit in the corner, I'll bring it over. I do and he does, double for a single, pricewise, 'cos of me injuries, see, 'cos he feels for me, gives me empathy.

I sit.
I sit and I sip.

I think.
I scratch a bit.

A woman comes in the pub, arm in a cast, all writin' on it, Jaysus, stitches in her face, carryin' messages. Plonks at the bar, orders a gin an' tonic.

Think about Ladyboy.

Some people say when he was born, his oul' dear threw away the body an' raised the afterbirth.

Some say he's called Ladyboy 'cos of an ingrown flute.

Was a Frenchman, Pierre, Ladyboy taught him one sentence, Kick me in the nuts, told him it meant Where's the toilet?, an' people bein' what they are . . .

Pierre confronted Ladyboy over it, pointed at him like that.

Pointed. Jabbed.

As Ladyboy opened wide, just before he took these two fingers off at the knuckles, Pierre swore he saw three sets of teeth instead of one.

Like a shark.

People fear The Ladyboy.

Rich Dave McGee an' Ladyboy're close enough, they buy each other gifts. Last year, Dave's visit home, he got Ladyboy betas. A red beta an' a blue beta.

Last week, I bumped into Ladyboy in the street, few lads crouched 'round a clear bucket of betas, these little fish that's supposed to fight, supposed to knock each other's blocks off.

Ladyboy tells us the fishes're from Siam, which is Thailand an' they fight them like cockfightin'.

He's tryin' to get them to fight stylish, so's he can put on a show for McGee at his annual bash down Canal way, the edge of the mountain, way of respect, a show of thanks.

Betas, they're called, says Ladyboy. Chink fightin' fish.
Chink meanin' Oriental.

But Ladyboy's gettin' pissed off, the fish won't fight.
Prods them with a wooden spoon, tryin' to agitate them, but they're lazy little fucks, one of them's a big stringy poo hangin' out it's hole, wants to be left in peace.

Watchin' Ladyboy an' his wooden spoon.
Got this itch, don't know where it came from.
Down in me shoe, under me foot, got me finger stuck in there, Ladyboy prods the red fish, down the side, there, I'm standin' on one foot, hoppin' a bit, balancin', prods it again, I scratch hardo, itchin's intense, I get bumped.

Slightly.

Softly.

But hard enough I topple over fuckways, hit the bucket and the betas bolt. Fishes flop in the grass, Ladyboy's livid, everyone panics, fuck're the fishes? stompin' around, the fishes're fucked, man, crushed underfoot.

Flat.

Dead.

Ladyboy looks at me.

Tells me if I don't want me kneecaps gone, seven hundred quid, I'm to pay him for his betas. For new ones. 'Cos that's how much they cot. Bring it to Dave McGee's, to his party, so Dave can meet the fuckhead who crushed his gift to his good friend, The Ladyboy.

Scared, 'cos tonight's the night, sip of me double, burney down, nerve tampin' taste, tonight's the night, this party.

Be there.

Be there or I will shoot you in the knee caps an' they will be gone.
An' you will not be able to walk properly for all the days.

Be there with the money.

I've gone to everyone I know. I've borrowed and wheedled all I can, everyone tells me to fuck off. Oul'fella was me last chance.

I've no mates.
No mates, I've only birds I shagged.
Went to all the birds I shagged, birds think I'm it. Got two hundred quid.

Need five hundred more.

Think.
Think.
Take a sip.
Think.

I don't know what to do.

Maybe I deserve what I get for . . . No, for nothin', I didn't,
I never did anything that bad. I never hurt anyone.
Maybe a couple of dollys.
Emotionally.
Unintentionally.

Sup of whiskey, big sup, brainstorm.
Brainstorm, brainstorm, think.

Woman at the bar orders another gee an' tee, it's only two
minutes after the first, perched there hunky, her plastic Spar
bags around the stool.

She turns to me, says, 'cos I'm the only one else in the bar,
says, me painkillers . . .
Eh . . . Sorry?
Me painkillers, she says. They make me drowsy.
Do they? I says.
Make me sleepy, she says, the fuckin' nutcase, all broken up.
Betcha her husband battered her or somethin', told her, Get
out there. Get the fuckin' shoppin'. Get me some grub to put
in me . . .

Idea.
Ah-hah.
Idea.

Up an' out. Up an' out of there.
Off.
Off to Ashbrook.

I'm off to Ashbrook, see this dolly I met last night, dolly who's
into me. She's money, she's savin', if I can charm the ninnies
off her, then borrow the *money* off her. In between, maybe
knock the *arse* off her . . .

I know she lives in Ashbrook but I don't know where.
Know she works checkout in a Spar, see that woman's
shoppin' bag reminded me.
Know she goes home for her lunch, know she's no car.
Deduce she walks.
Deduce she works where she lives.

Gonna investigate. Find a Spar in Ashbrook, find her there.

Headin' through the Close, spot The Howie Lee, Peaches' mate 'cross the green, sittin' on a bench, smokin'.

Howie that held me for a batterin'.

He spots me, stands up, he shouts.
I turn.
He calls me name.
I'm gone.
I'm gone up The Limekiln lane.

Go the long way, take me twice as long, now, balls! Get there before one anyway.
Slow down, now, I'm safe.

Relax.

Left him for dust, I did.

Look for, can't find, *find* it. Find the Spar, hope me deduction's right, inside, blonde haired dolly bird – next please – *is* right.

Fuck she get the big plaster on her head?

Sidle up, say Hello. D'you wanna meet?
Lunch, she says.
Your place?
Yes, she says. 'Cos she's *into* me, see.

Fifteen minutes wait, compare Baxters soup to Campbells, pricewise, healthwise, kills time.
Baxters' best, it's not condensed.

Let's go, we go, her gaff.
Hop on her. Me brother, she says, he's in school.
So?
He comes home for lunch.
Oh. Kiss her mouth, We'll tell him we're wrestlin' or somethin'.
Kiss her tongue, We'll tell him we're playin' the Gladiators.

Ninnies off, get her nippy.
She keeps kissin' me wounds. They turn her on to bits.

Lodgy-bodgy hard. Come quick, a post coital caress, she deserves it, we dress.

Microwave lasagne, tasty, come to the point.

Lend me money.

Why?
I owe it.
What makes you think I have it?

Best of banter, back an'forth, finish grub, nam, nam, lully, liked it.

That money you said you were savin' for your brother's school. His special school. Whatsit, a month's?
Six, she says.
Six month's tuition. Lend me the money an' I will tutor him meself. I will teach him, not only Peter an' Jane an' Spot the dog, but I will teach him the facts of life. I will teach him the manly things of how to survive in a world of pain, made doubly worse 'cos he's slow.

You know nothing of manly things, she says, you know nothin' 'cos you run away from people in pubs.

Sore point, me lack of manliness, so it slips out.
Cunt.
Get out, she says.
Thanks for the lodgy.
. . . An' fuck you, she says.

Not too well handled, that. Bit rubbish.
See, I shouldn't've rode her yet. The ride should've been the carrot I dangled.
But I'm not leavin' yet. Stand me ground, I'm gonna persuade.

Call her a cunt again.
Get out!
Cunt! (Can't help it.)
Out! she says.

Key in the door, bollox, the brother.

Calm it, quiet, don't wanna scare the fucker, might give him the idea I'm dangerous.

Steps into the room, he's six foot tall, built like a human white puddin', looks inbred.

I wanna tousle his hair, some reason.

Opens his mouth, he can't talk too well. Figures, 'cos of his face, his moon face, he's a, whatchacall, which?
Down syndrome, she says.
The poor fucker, I say. Not tryin' to . . . Well. Yeah. *Tryin'* to be a funny cunt.

Get him, she says.

Out of the blue, he roundhouses me in the face, rings me ears baddo, knocks me into the wall. Stagger 'round, tryin' to get me sea legs, another roundhouse, awkward as fuck, like a dolly's dig, but powerful, much more powerful than The Peaches' was, knocks me down, it does. I hear her through the din in me ears, the ringin'.

That's one thing I do not stand for, she says. I do not stand people givin' my brother the mock.

I can't believe this. Second time I've got the bates in two days an' what've I to look forward to tonight?
Another one.
Another, probably the worst.
Probably the worst batin' ever.

Me stereo! she squeaks, I'm tumblin' over it, landin' in a hape.

Have to do somethin', now, I'm thinkin', get out the door, *somethin'*. C'mon, now, The Rookie. Shake me head like in the funnies, the ringin' lessens, head clears a bit.
But, he's blockin' the door.
He's blockin' the door an' he's purple.
Only one way out, has to be done. One way, the only way.
Better than facin' the white puddin' boy, now gone purple.

Look 'round, spot the stereo.

Nobody gives my brother the mock, she says.

Pick up the stereo, *Me stereo!!!!* fuck it through the window.

Follow it through, Dive. Dive. Dive.

Then tuck.
Tuck, roll, I hit the deck, glass in me back and follow through
to me feet. Nicely judged, that, now run.

Front of me, bollox.

Front of me, The Howie. The Howie Lee, blockin' me escape.

Turn back, run into the puddin' boy, he gets me in a neck grab,
squeezes. Air's trapped, brain's cut off from oxygen an' blood,
feel meself gettin' dizzy. See your one lookin' at me through
the window, cryin', me stereo! Over an' over. Me stereo! Feel
me consciousness, slippin' . . . slippin' . . . slippin' . . .

Bam! Then, I'm dropped.
All a sudden, dropped, coughin' up gook, me throatpipe's all
throttled.

Bam! Bam! I look up, The Howie's layin' into the puddin' boy,
plantin' punch after punch on his stomach an' ribs, poundin'
double quick, flurrious furious combos, weakens the middle
area, starts throwin' head shots, snappin' it back like that. Bam!
Bam! Snap back. Bam! Down to the ribs, I hear a crack,
Jaysus, he's a goer. White puddin' boy may as well be on
Mars, he's grabbin', graspin' at the air, while The Howie bobs
an' ducks, hooks, jabs an' chops, chops, chops the jolly giant
down.

No problem to him a-tall.

Easy as pie.

Puddin' boy sits in the grass all stunned, The Howie bends
over him, gives his hair a little tousle, he starts whingein',
callin' his ma, the sis comes out – only he's callin' the *sis* ma –
and hugs him, holds him.

The *sis* is ma.

Ah, here, now.

Too ashamed of her son to call him son, calls him brud, did
you ever hear the fuckin' like?!

You all right? he asks me, The Howie.

I can't answer, 'cos now *he's* tears tumblin' down his face as
well, makin' hic-hic noises, sobbin'.

The fuck's everyone cryin' for?

You all right? he says.
Are *you?* I say.
Asks me what the fuck I'm talkin' about.

Headin' off a short cut back road, wee-wah, wee-wah, coppers?
Coppers for us? Coppers for the scrap? The smashed window?
Comin' to nab us?
Wee-wah, closer.

In a bush, this bush, down. Crouch an' observe. The Howie's
still sobbin'.
Corner in eyeshot, wee-wah's closer.

Any second.

Any second.

Over the bushes linin' the road, down at the turn, I see
somethin' movin', somethin' red, hoverin' along the tops,
comin' towards the bend.

Whatsit? Whatsit? Reveal yourself.

An' it's Flann Dingle's van, Ginger Boy on top, doin' sixty,
tools past fasto, kicks up dust in our faces, followed by Gardamobile, wee-wah, hot, hot, hot pursuit, copper intent on capture.

Stop at the primary school, we perch on the steps, he stops
sobbin', starts talkin', he's sorry. Wants to help me. Won't tell
me why. Just does.

Feel sorry for the bloke.

Says he wants to make up to me what he done to me.
Say he already has.
Says he hears I'm in trouble.
Who told you?
A birdie.
A birdie?
A dirty birdie, that cunt set the puddin' boy on you told me last
night.

Don't be angry, he says. I didn't actually *do* anything with her.

All contrite, like, as if I could do anything 'bout it anyway.

Tell me your woes, he says. Tell me your woes 'bout the fishes
an' I will help you.
You know about the fishes? I says.
I believe there's fishes involved, he says.

So, I tell him me woes an' he helps me.

He helps me a way I don't understand.

Me itchin's bad, man, me ribs hurt, I can feel me eye, me
bruised eye throbbin' from where I was battered, but feel me
itchin' worse, it's another sort of pain.

Asks me why I'm itchin'. Tell him I don't know why, but I'm
dyin' scratchin'. Asks me what do I know about the scabies?

Who're they? I says.

Come with me, he says.

Takes me to the chemists, buys me a gift, some ointment. Tells
me to put it all over me body, bollox, hole an' all , leave it for
a day. Don't wash an' it won't itch any more.

How do you know? I say.
'Cos I do, he says.

It's all a bit fuckin' mysterious.

Saves me bacon, cures me ills, astounds me.

I go all introspective an' pond'rous for a minute.

I will help you with The Ladyboy, he says. Out of the blue.
I will help you with The dirtbird Ladyboy.

Like he read me fuckin' mind.

Like a fuckin'. . . a fortune teller.

Then he reaches out an' touches me bruised eye. Gently.
Gently. Not gay, like, just . . . And then he puts his hand once
through me hair, like that, starin' at me like he's thinkin' 'bout
somethin' else.

Home, shower, ointment, all over, even crevices. It stinks. I won't smell too attractive at the party tonight. Doesn't matter. I'll be there on business.
Comb me hair carefully, all the same. Dress neat, dress nice, look in the mirror long.

Habits die hard, I'm stylish.

Me wounds.
Startin' to stop hurtin'. Stop hurtin' baddo, start lookin' goodo.
Look like a warrior, I do.
All right, there, love? I say, practisin'. Habits die hard.
All right there love?

Me voice trembles like a pansy's.

Meet down the fort. Whiskeys, high stools, The Howie leans forward, gives me a good sniff, nods, says, Good man.

I tells him I'm still itchy. He says, Patience, man, it doesn't happen straight away.

I ask him how we're gonna deal with The Ladyboy? Doesn't tell me.

Won't.

Tells me a story instead.

Huddle.
Huddle in.
Huddle an' hark.

Had to collect his little brud, name's Mousey from playschool one day. Homeward, had to take him by the primary school. Stopped for a gander, kids on their breaks, horsin' in the yard.

Next year, you'll be in there, he tells the brud.
Will I? says the brud.
You will, says The Howie.

Youngfella strolls over the gate, youngfella, seven or eight. Hello, says The Howie. Youngfella spits a gozzy on the brud, no reason, greener in his face, runs away back into the yard.

Three o'clock, hometime, The Howie stalks the school, follows the youngfella home. Youngfella goes in, has his dinner, comes

out to play. Meantime, The Howie's after collectin' the brud,
The Mouse, bringin' him back up. Goes over the youngfella,
throws him on the ground an' gives him a clatter, holds him there
by the ears. Tells The Mouse to get the biggest biliest, snottiest
fuckin' gozzy he can an' drop it into the youngfella's face.

The Mouse does.

Sticky green thing.

Youngfella doesn't like it a'tall.

Why tell me this? I says.
Cos . . . Puts his fingers up, two pints, like that, two pints, two
whiskeys, 'cos I wanted to tell you about me an' The Mouse.
Nice one, says I. Nice one.
Pints an' shorts on the bar.
To The Mouse, says The Howie, pint in the air.
Nice one, says I. Hoist mine high.

Road to rich McGee's.

Sun's goin' down, a warm night comin' on, see Flann Dingle
an' Ginger boy pass by perpendicular, slowly now, not
followed, Ginger boy sittin' on the roof.

Somethin' sparks in me head.
Somethin' to do with Flann Dingle an' Ginger boy.
Sparks but doesn't ignite.

It'll come to me, some stage.

Getting' the butterflies, now. Startin' to taste pennies an'
twopences, the unknown, The Howie Lee versus Ladyboy, me
in the middle. Have to trust him things'll be okay.

Hard to trust when I'm brickin', but then, he saved me today,
saved me bacon.
An' he knew things, knew how to stop me itchin'.
Even now it's less.

So I kind of believe in him.

Hear the music 'fore we see the gaff. Two gaffs made into one,
detached, people millin' outside, lights, coloured lights out the
window, laughin', happy.

Taste of copper in me mouth gets stronger, the adrenaline.

Halitosis in the air. Feel it more than smell it.
Howie wrinkles his nose.
He feels it too.

An' it dawns on me.
Flann Dingle. Flann Dingle, the hi-ace an' The Ginger boy.
The Mayans.
Been seein' them all day, too much, too many times.
Thinkin' 'bout death comin', form of a green hi-ace.
Comin' to get me.

Approach.

Approach an' in, party business, masses of cunts lookin' dandy.

Who's that? That's not . . . I think it is. I think it's Matt. Matt
Dillon, the actor. Dave McGee must be mates with the stars an'
all, now, Matt in his long black coat, smokin' a fat cigar like
the superstar he isn't, hasn't hacked it decent in years, fuckin'
dollys millin' 'round him.

Bump into The Chopper Al.

Hi, Chopper Al, says The Howie, sounds like he's sayin' the
High Chapperal.

Last I saw of *you*, you were after *him*, Chopper says to The
Howie. Points at me.
We're the buds now, says The Howie. Did you see The
Ladyboy?
Why? says the Chopper.

'Cos now I'm after *him*.

Chopper Al says nothin'.

Chopper Al goes white, backs off, disappears.

An' like that, so does me fear.

In, around, no sign of The Ladyboy, one room, another, no
sign, stairs, up them.

Spot Matt down in the hallway, Matt, I shouts. Matt.
He looks up an' I have to say it.

You've lost it, man.
What's that, buddy? Big grin on his puss.
Give it up, man, I says. It's no use.
Brown sauce face, he knows *exactly* what I'm talkin' 'bout.

Matt Dillon, the brown sauce man.

Up the stairs, check three rooms, into a fourth, bare, wooden floorboards, spacious.
An' who's there only The Ladyboy. Ladyboy an' Dave McGee, best of mates, heads close, whisperin', couple of conspirin' cunts.

Ah-hem.

That's The Howie.

Ah-hem.

Clearin' his throat loud, Ladyboy looks at me an' me fear comes back quadruplo.
All right, bud? he says. Have you got me money for me dearly departed, for me fightin' betas?

Don't know what to say.

. . . Or do I have to wreck your knees, turn you into a gammy boy?

Fuck do I say?

Well . . .?

I fart.
A hot one.
Deep an' loooud.
Just comes out with the fear, me hole's instinct to void itself.

Everyone goes quiet. The smell wafts across the room. It's like we're waitin' 'til it reaches The Ladyboy's nostrils.

They quiver.
Once. Twice.

So it's like that? he says.

Mustn't've liked it.

I'm sorry to hear you take that attitude.

All right, Ladyboy?

The Howie.

All right, Ladyboy?

An' The Ladyboy's lookin' at The Howie now an his eyes're squintin' 'cos The Howie's here an' The Howie has a bit of a rep himself.

Howie's rep is, an' everyone knows this, he's a goer goes all the way.

Key in the door, The Howie turns, locks it, puts it in his pocket, turns back to The Ladyboy.

An' then his fists clench.
An' his veins knot.
An' he rocks on his heels.

Back . . . an' forth. Back . . . an' forth. Back . . . an' forth.

An' Ladyboy takes off his coat, folds it on the windowsill.

An' no-one says anything 'cos nothin' *needs* to be said.

An' back . . . an' forth The Howie rocks.

Dave McGee backs to the wall.

I back to the other wall.

An' The Ladyboy bends his knees, his body goes all springy.

There's ladies an' gents, I can hear them, arriving outside the door. The Chopper Al's been talkin', spreadin' the ska.

The Howie Lee versus The Ladyboy an' no-one'll see it.
No one 'cept me an' Dave McGee.

Me bowels an' bladder feel all open inside me.

An' all becomes quiet as they look at each other intense an' hungry, their jaws all knotted up; patient like boxers waitin' on the bell.

I fart again.

An' they go for each other.

An' there's boxin' an' punchin' an' it's excitin' stuff.

Circle, a skirmish an' part, circle, a skirmish an' part.

Good technique an' strategy.

But then, stances are dropped, just like that, closed hands open an' the snarlin' starts.

Jabs an' uppercuts, feints an' parrys are abandoned as useless, traded for tearin' an' pumellin' an' cuts an' eye flaps hangin' an' groin shots over an' over.

I nearly go.

I nearly piss meself.

'Cos it's not normal fisticuffs any more, not Marquis of Queensberry.
It's blood an' bone.

An' no more nearly, I *do* piss meself, hardly notice.

A vision of blood an' teeth, right there, of skin an' hair an' they're flyin' so fast 'round the room, I'm afraid if they touch off me, I'll scald, I'll burn.

A bangin' on the door outside.

Fuck off.

Shoutin' an' poundin'.

They wanna come in, see the berserkers brainin' each other, hear bones poppin' an' crackin'.

Well, they can't. Fuck them.

Ladyboy bites The Howie right through his face, snaps again for a better grip an' shakes him 'round on a rubbery neck, tearin'.

Comes away with a piece of red an' white in his mouth, spits it all juicy.

Red freckles spot Dave McGee's face an' rich as he is, he vomits an' faints.

Time passes real slow.

Me piss is cold on me legs.

Pummelin' gets louder from outside.

An' on they go.

An' on they go.

Stop.

An' then they stop.

They pause an' circle, two of them are breathin' hard, but it doesn't sound right, 'cos noses've been snapped, the air's goin' in an' out fuckways.

An' I can see the white, the horrible white of The Howie's snaggle tooth through his cheek, a dirty gobbet hangin'.

Ladyboy's left leg's exposed, his trousers ripped from crotch to foot. White foam seethes out between his teeth an' bubbles.

Somethin' heavy's bangin' against the door outside.

They're both a shambles, but their eyes're black an' smokin'.

They go again an' so do I, a warm flood.

Howie smacks Ladyboy's head off the wall, leavin' a blood an' hair stain.

Ladyboy's head snaps forward, teeth poppin', poppin' at Howie's neck, walks into a poleaxin' right.

An' on like this.
They're still goin', still tradin' damage back an' forth, I'm getting' used to skin on skin sounds.

But gettin' a bit slower now.

Slower an' slower.

Both cryin', I think, a weird kinda keenin' sound.

They're windin' down.

Exhausted.

The odd bandy punch, or misaimed kick, an accidental clash of heads.

An' slower still.

'Til Ladyboy, knackered, his bein' the weaker flesh; spent, spent like seed, like spunk, sinks to the floor, sits, then lies down.

An' the door comes crashin' in, crushed by a beer-keg batterin' ram.

Too late.

The Howie walks by me an' out, doesn't even look at me.

Huge crowd, there, reaches all the way down the stairs out the street, quiet, now. Watchin' him. Howie limps buckled to the end of the landin' away from the stairs.
Crowd scuttles sideways like a clutch of crabs to let him through.
He sits down against the jacks door.

His head's down. I can't see his face.

We watch.

We listen to his strange, fucked up breathin'.

Ruination.

An' way, way in the distance, I'm sure I hear a siren.

Knocked sideways, fuck is that?
Three bods march along the landin', knockin' people aside, three bods I know.
Ollie Murphy, The Peaches an' The Peaches' monstrous sister, Avalanche.
Down the end of the hall, Peaches picks poor Howie, tired Howie up.
Him an' Ollie hold him there.
Hold him, tell him, how dare he? How dare he presume to fuck The Peaches' sister? How dare he fuck her an' dump her like a dirty toerag? Behind The Peaches' back? Makin' her think someone loved her when she was unloveable? Givin' her hope?

See his face, now, his expression, a man come to the end of somethin'.

Are youse after me, lads? he says.

An' they pull him sideways an' run him into the jacks an' towards the window, an' out he goes, screams an' shouts, but doesn't fly.

Doesn't fly, drops.

Music stops an' I run downstairs, me an' everyone else an' out the front door an' a crowd, push me way, get in there, see me mate, see The Howie, The *good* Howie on the railin's, spike through his back an' out his shoulder, teeth showin' through his cheek, wretched.

Wretched.

An' we stand an' we watch an' he smiles an' I know why, it's 'cos he looks so ridiculous an' all's still an'quiet.

All right? I says to him.
All right, he says. Are you itchin?
An' I'm not. Didn't notice, but haven't itched all night.
No, I say.
That's the cream, he says. It's beginnin' to work.

An' listen.

Listen, the distance.

A siren.

Faint. Then closer.

Ambulance an' fire brigade comin' to cut The Howie off the railin's, make him better.
An' everyone, same idea, backs up to make room, leaves a gap for the emergency boys to drive on in.

An' louder gets the siren an' here comes the emergency boys, only it's not the firemen an' it's not the ambulance, it's Flann Dingle an' Ginger boy, powerin' the hi-ace 'round the corner, doin' ninety, siren's the gards in hot pursuit, Ginger boy's on his hunkers, clingin' to the roof-rack.

An' Flann should turn off here, but he doesn't, maybe can't an' he powers ahead, straight forward, straight for The Howie an' two hundred people turn their heads away, all together, all at once an' squeeze their eyes shut.

An' as I close mine, that last moment, I'm sure I see – I'm positive – the Howie's body come apart by itself, just before the two tons of metal slams into him, me mate, me new, me impaled mate, me namesake the name of Lee, me saviour, an', eyes closed, I can hear the sound of metal grindin', metal of the hi-ace, metal of the railin's an' I can't open me eyes, 'til the gardamobile does a movie skid an' a fellacopper an' a slappercopper get out an' go 'round the front of the mangled hi-ace where no-one else'll go.

An' the slappercopper comes back white, starin', shakin'.

An' the fellacopper comes back cryin'.

There's another body there, he tells the slappercopper. There's two bodies. The impaled boy and the boy with the ginger hair, went off the roof.

Look in the van, the slappercopper says.
You.
No, you. I'm not goin' near it.

An' they argue on about who's gonna look in on Flann an' I skeddadle 'cos I can't take it.

Walk along thinkin' 'bout how maybe the Mayan god of death appeared to The Howie, not me. Appeared to The Howie in the form of the Ginger boy . . .
and Flann Dingle . . .
and the green hi-ace van.

End up outside The Howie's, somehow, Howie's oul one's an' oul'fella's gaff, got an urge, an urge to yak, to knock in an' give them the ska. Tell them the story of The Howie's death.

Let them know he was good at the end.

Stand there, watchin'.
Watch there, thinkin'.
Knowin' I won't go home, go anywhere 'til I do this.

So up I go, a rap on the door, a man answers.

Can I come in? They don't know.
What's it about?
The Howie. They don't know yet.
Come in, he says, you're very photogenic, he says.

I've somethin' of importance to tell you, I says.
Well, in that case, I'll go fetch Mrs Lee, he says.
That might be best, I says, puts me in the sittin' room to wait.

Sit down, telly's on, some kind of video, home video.

Young boy in a suit.
Little boy, five or six years old.
Sittin' where I'm sittin' on the sofa.

Hand comes into the frame, steadies his shoulder, stays there.

The boy's face is grey.

His eyes are on mine.

His expression doesn't change.